A New True Book

ELEPHANTS

By Elsa Posell

*This "true book" was prepared
under the direction of
Illa Podendorf,
formerly with the Laboratory School,
University of Chicago*

CHILDRENS PRESS, CHICAGO

Elephant

True Book of Elephants

PHOTO CREDITS

Art Thoma—Cover
Lynn M. Stone—2, 4, (top), 6, 10, 11, 14 (left), 20
James P. Rowan—4 (bottom)
Candee & Associates—44 (right)
H. Melzacher—9, 14 (right), 16, 27 (right), 33 (left),
41, 42 (2 photos), 44 (left), 45
Julie O'Neil—12, 21
Chandler Forman—18, 22, 25, 27 (left), 31, 35, 37
Louise Lunak—28, 33 (right), 39
COVER—African elephant,
        Washington, D.C., Zoo

Library of Congress Cataloging in Publication Data

Posell, Elsa Z.
  Elephants.
  (A New true book)
  Revised edition of: The true book of elephants. 1964.
  Summary: An introduction to Indian and African
elephants, including what they eat, how they live, and
how they are captured and tamed.
  1. Elephants—Juvenile literature.
[1. Elephants] I. Title.
QL737.P98P67   1982   599.6′l   81-38470
ISBN 0-516-01621-0   AACR2

TABLE OF CONTENTS

African elephant

Asian, or Indian, elephant

WHERE DO THEY COME FROM?

When you see elephants at the zoo, do you wonder where they come from?

They come from either Africa or Asia.

Asian elephants come from Sri Lanka, Sumatra, Burma, Thailand, and India. Asian elephants are sometimes called Indian elephants.

A baby elephant may be born at the zoo, but its parents or grandparents came from a jungle far away.

HOW MANY KINDS ARE THERE?

There are two kinds of elephants—African and Asian.

Asian elephants are smaller than African elephants. Their ears are smaller. Their tusks are smaller. Sometimes they have no tusks at all.

These elephants can be trained to do many jobs. They push and carry heavy trees. At times they carry people. Asian, or Indian, elephants can carry or pull heavier loads than any other work animal.

Elephants in the circus are almost always Indian elephants.

WHAT ARE THEY LIKE?

Elephants are the largest
of all land animals. An
elephant may weigh as
much as sixty men.

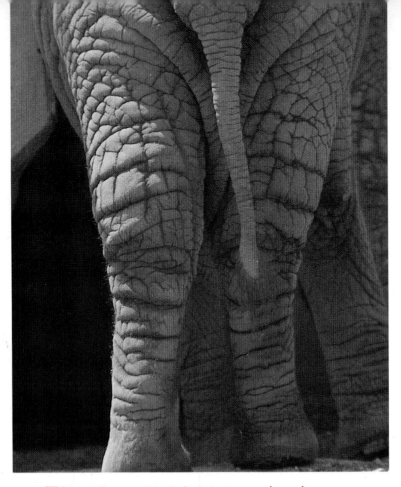

Even though its skin is thick, an elephant can feel a fly land on its back.

Elephants have dark gray skin about an inch thick. There is little hair on an elephant's hide, but its long tail ends in a tuft of wiry hair.

Because it is so big, an elephant has legs that are like thick, strong posts. Elephants have small eyes and do not see well.

African elephants have big ears.

They spread their large
ears to catch sounds. They
lift their long trunks to
catch the smells that tell
them of danger, or where
to find food or other
members of the herd.

An elephant's trunk is part of its nose and top lip. It has nostrils at the end of it. It is almost six-feet long.

The trunk is a tube with a tab like a finger at the end of it. An African elephant has two tabs at the end of its trunk.

An elephant uses these tabs as we use our fingers. It touches and feels things with them.

A thirsty elephant draws water into its trunk. Then it blows the water into its mouth.

When flies are biting, an elephant may give itself a shower. It fills its trunk with sand or mud and blows it all over its huge body.

Elephants take care of their trunks. Sometimes they curl them up to protect them from danger.

Both male and female African elephants can have long tusks. Indian elephants have tusks, too, but the female's tusks will only be two inches long.

An elephant's tusks are two overgrown front teeth. Tusks of an African elephant may be over six feet long and weigh a hundred pounds each.

WHAT DO THEY EAT?

Elephants need lots of food.

They travel far to find grass, plants, leaves, roots, and fruits.

Elephants travel mostly at night. During the hot days they stay close to water and rest a great deal.

Elephants only sleep two or three hours at a time.

Some elephants sleep standing up. Others roll on their sides to sleep.

As they move through forests, elephants knock down young trees to get the tender leaves. They dig up trees with their tusks and eat the roots.

Elephants chew or grind their food with four teeth that can be twelve inches long.

In time these teeth are worn down. New teeth that have grown in behind the old ones take their place.

An elephant grows six sets of teeth. A new set does not move into place until the old set is worn down.

As a special treat an elephant may get a bucket of potatoes, apples, carrots, or fruit.

It is a big job to feed an elephant. In one day a grown elephant in a zoo may eat 150 pounds of hay, 100 pounds of leaves, 10 loaves of bread, and some grain.

HOW DO THEY LIVE?

Elephants live in families, or herds. There may be ten elephants in a herd, or there may be a hundred or more.

African elephants in Uganda

African elephants with young in Kenya

The mother elephant is called a cow. The father elephant is called a bull. Baby elephants are called calves.

Each herd has a leader. The leader is usually the smartest female in the herd. The leader walks ahead when the herd moves. The cows and calves come next, and then the bulls.

When there is danger, the bulls form a circle around the cows and calves to protect them.

A mother elephant has only one baby at a time. Its skin is light gray and covered with black hair, which it soon loses.

When the calf is one day old, it can stand up. A calf may weigh over two hundred pounds and be three feet tall.

Like all babies, the elephant calf is hungry. It soon finds its mother's milk and drinks and drinks. A calf drinks about twenty quarts of its mother's milk in one day.

The mother stays close to her calf. She often wraps it in her long trunk.

When the baby is about three days old, it follows its mother to where the herd is feeding.

The elephants look at the calf and pat it with their trunks. Then they squeal a welcome.

A mother elephant takes good care of her baby. The calf stays close to its mother and drinks her milk until it is three or four years old.

Baby elephants stay close to their mothers.

The mother shows her
calf where to find leaves,
grass, and other kinds of
food. She shows it how to
keep away from danger.

If a calf does not
behave, she spanks it with
her trunk.

Mother elephants help each other take care of baby elephants.

Baby elephants play games and tricks on each other. Sometimes they hold on to each other's tails and march like soldiers.

A tired calf may hang on to its mother's tail and be pulled along.

Baby elephants grow more than two inches every year. They are full grown when they are sixteen or eighteen years old. But they continue to grow until they are thirty years old.

Elephants are old when they are sixty or seventy years old. They live about as long as people do.

African elephants at a river in Kenya. Do you see the giraffe in the background?

Elephants are gentle.
They live at peace with
each other.
The whole herd may
stay with an elephant that
is sick or hurt.

If the herd must move on, a few elephants are left to care for the sick one until it is well.

As a herd travels, there are rest stops for mothers and their babies who get tired.

Grown-up elephants are good swimmers. They seem to enjoy a splash in a river.

Elephants like to take baths.

Even though they are so big, elephants can move through a forest without making a sound.

However, when frightened, they start to run and push. They make so much noise that they can be heard many miles away.

WHO IS AN ELEPHANT'S ENEMY?

In the wilds of its home, a grown elephant is bigger and stronger than any other animal. People are the elephant's only real enemy.

Elephant tusks are made of ivory.

Many elephants have been killed for their ivory tusks. These can be sold for money. Ivory is used to make handles, statues, billiard balls, jewelry, and many other things.

So many elephants were killed that it looked as if there would be none left.

People from all over the world wanted the elephants to be saved.

Laws have now been made to save the elephants.

A hunter must have a license. A hunter may not shoot mother elephants or their babies.

A hunter may hunt only in certain places.

Some places have been made safe for elephants. No hunting or capturing is allowed there.

Still much more must be done to save the elephants.

No hunting is allowed on this game preserve in Kenya.

HOW ARE THEY CAPTURED AND TAMED?

Sometimes a whole village takes part in an elephant hunt. The people work for weeks to build a large fenced pen. This is called a keddah.

A large herd of elephants is driven toward the pen.

Working elephants in Sri Lanka

Many villagers hide
along the path to the pen.
Suddenly the men begin to
beat drums, to whistle, and
to scream.

The frightened elephants start to run.

Suddenly torches are lighted. The elephants turn away from the torches. The only way for them to go is into the pen.

As soon as they are all in the pen, the huge gate is closed.

The elephants roar and push, but the fence is strong. The elephants are captured. After a few days, the gate is opened and some men on tame elephants go into the pen.

Tame elephants are used during an elephant hunt.

Indian elephants are trained
to do heavy work.

Old elephants and
mothers with calves are
set free. Only the strong,
young elephants are kept.

The tame elephants hold
the wild elephants down
while the men rope or
chain their legs.

The captured elephants are fed. They are given water. Then they are left alone with some tame elephants.

Soon young boys called oozies arrive. Each oozie works with one elephant.

He brings it a banana or some other fruit. He pats it and talks softly. The elephant learns to know his voice.

The boy works with
his elephant. The oozie
and the elephant become
friends. The elephant wants
to please the oozie. So
it obeys him.

At last the wild elephant
is tame and ready to work.

Not all tame elephants
do heavy work. Some are
sent to zoos and circuses.
That is where most people
in the world get to see
these wonderful animals.

WORDS YOU SHOULD KNOW

capture(CAP • cher) — to catch; to get hold of

herd — a group of animals that live together

hide(HYDE) — the skin of an animal

huge(HYOOJ) — very big

ivory(EYE • ver • ee) — smooth, hard, yellowish-white material that forms the elephant's tusk

keddah(KEH • dah) — a large fenced pen

license(LY • sense) — permission to do or own something

nostril(NAH • stril) — the outer opening of the nose

oozie(OO • zee) — a young boy who trains wild animals

plow — a farm machine that turns over soil

tab — a small flap on the end of something

tame(TAIM) — not dangerous; gentle

tender(TEN • dir) — soft; not tough

tuft — a small bunch of something held together tightly at one end and loose at the other

tusk — a long pointed tooth that comes outside of the mouth of some animals

wild — not under control

INDEX